This book belongs to:

_____

Start at the dots and trace over the dashes to the creature at the end of each line.

Start at the dots and trace over the dashes to the creature at the end of each line.

Start at the dots and trace over the dashes to the creature at the end of each line.

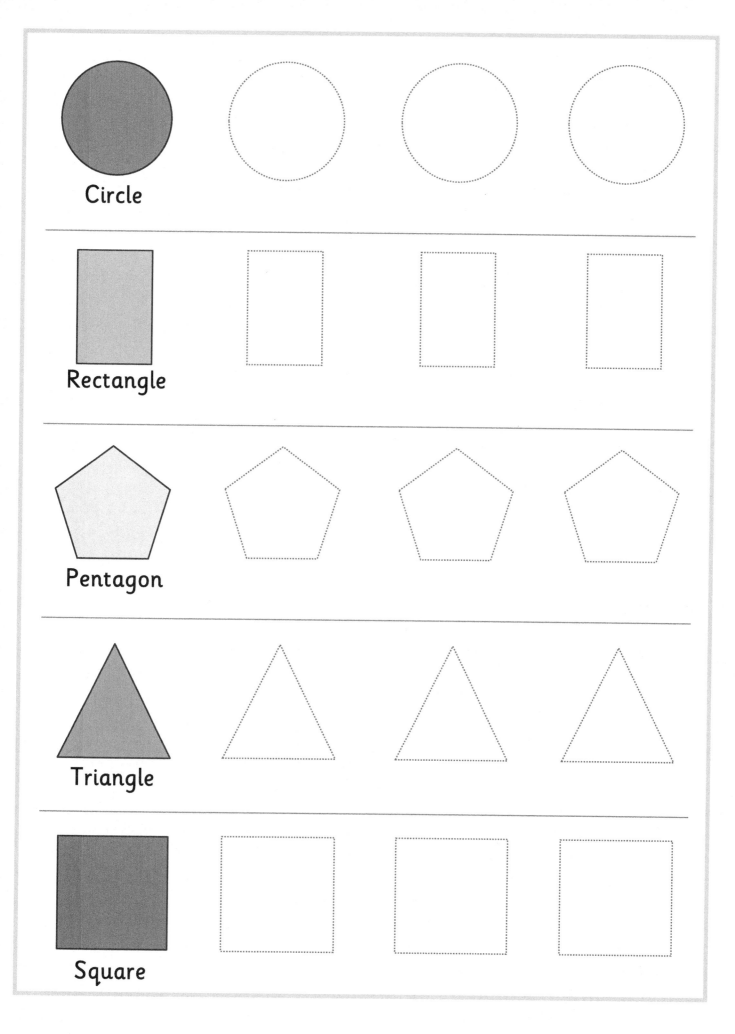

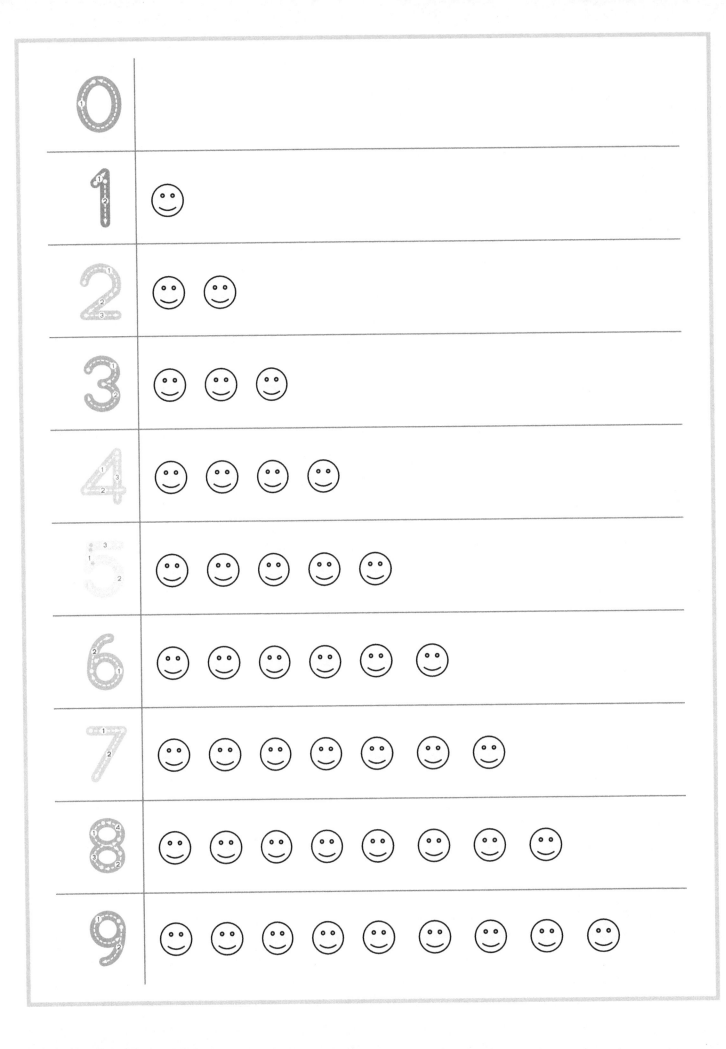

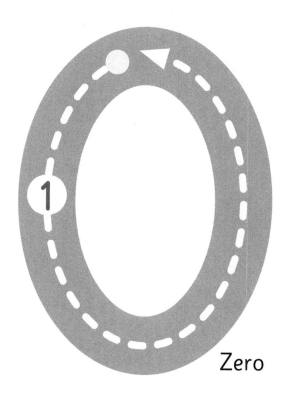

Zero

I see  hen.

One

I see  dongkys.

I see __3__ pigs.

Three

I see dogs.

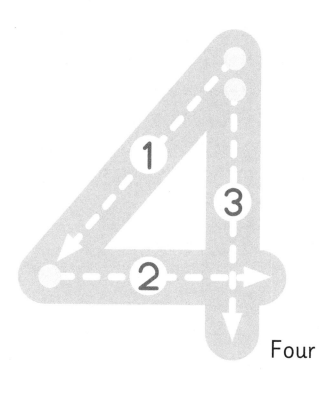

Four

I see ___ sheeps.

Five
5

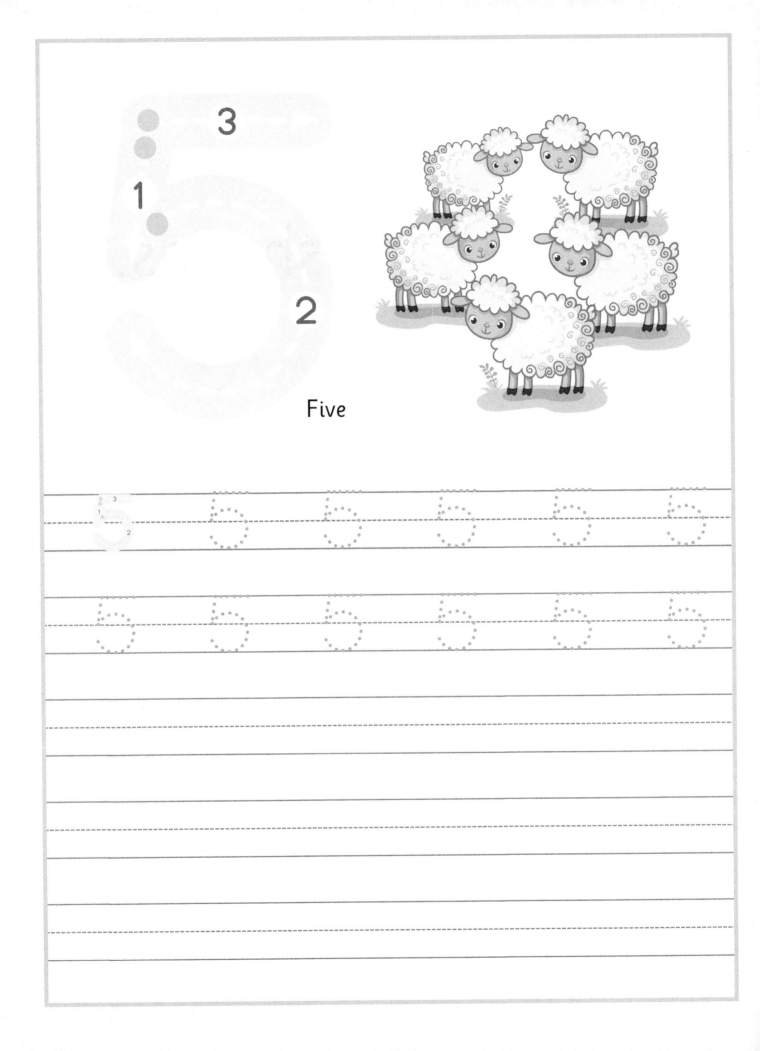

Five

I see  ducks.

Seven

I see cats.

I see  frogs.

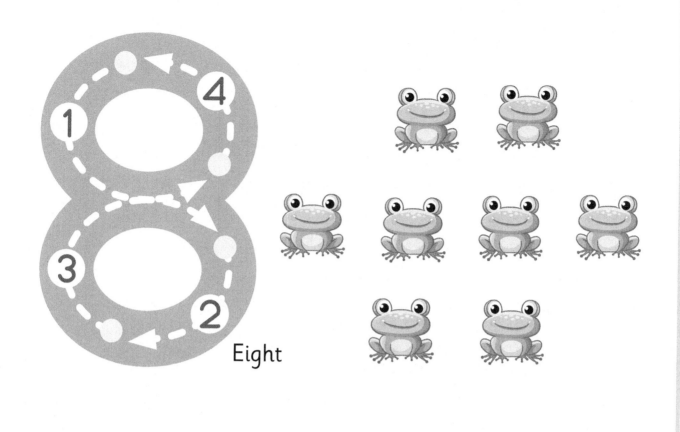

Eight

Nine

I see  goats.

Practice.

Count and Write the numbers.

Example

    3

   _____

 _____

 _____

Count and Write the numbers.

_____

_____

_____

_____

How many are there?
Match.

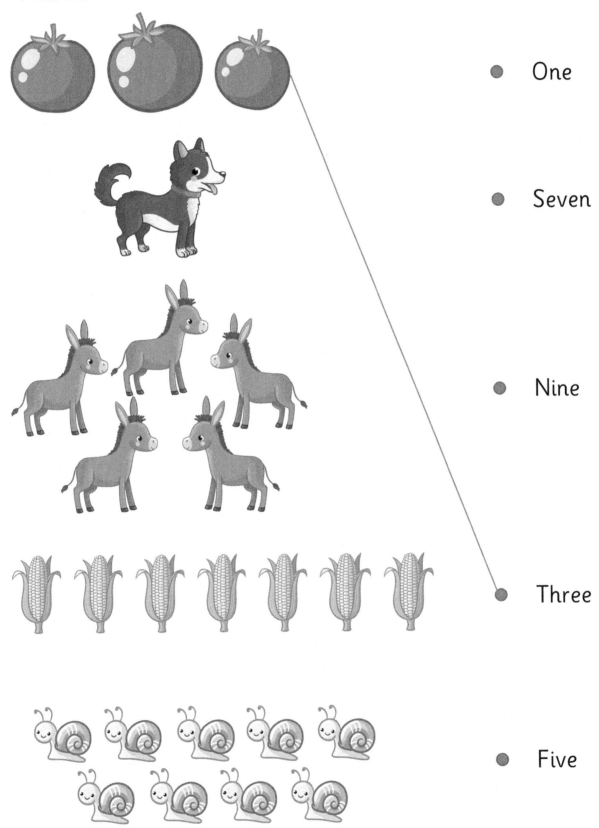

How many are there?
Match.

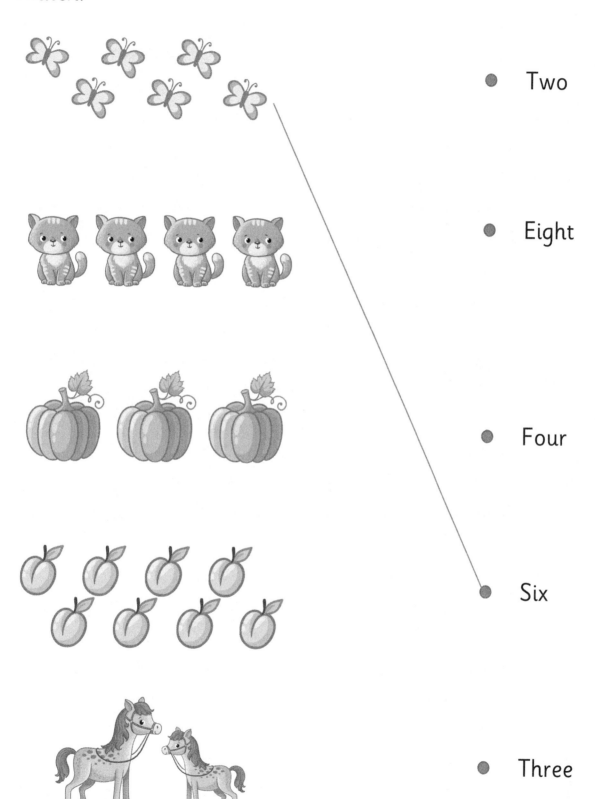

Count.

Circle the groups that show the same number.

Example

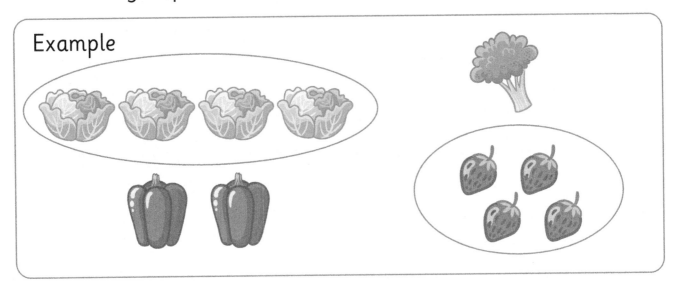

(a)

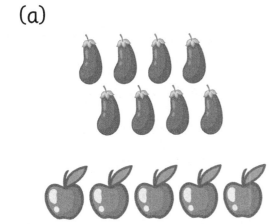

(b)

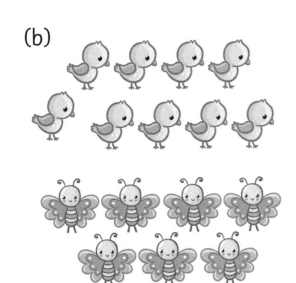

Count.

Circle the groups that show the same number.

(c)

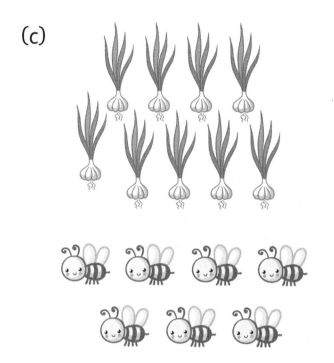

(d)

Count and Write the number.

_____

_____

_____

_____

What is 1 more? Write the number.

_____

_____

_____

What is 1 less? Write the number.

_____

_____

_____

Complete each number pattern.

Match.

- 10 — ten
- 0 — zero
- 7 — seven
- 2 — two
- 5 — five
- 9 — nine
- 4 — four

Match.

- 1 — one
- 6
- 4
- 3
- 8
- 5
- 9

- five
- four
- eight
- one
- nine
- three
- six

Made in the USA
Middletown, DE
06 February 2019